J OHN CHARLES DALY, former ABC News chief: This public policy forum, part of a series presented by the American Enterprise Institute, is concerned with the division of war powers between the Congress and the president. Our Founding Fathers, after much debate, preferred not to spell out that division precisely in the Constitution, but in the last three decades Congress has been determined to interpret and define it. Our subject: War Powers and the Constitution.

Many resolutions and bills have been exhaustively debated in Congress, and it is not extreme to say that the mountain has long labored and brought forth no consensus on precisely where war powers lie. The passage over President Nixon's veto of the War Powers Resolution of 1973 served principally to establish a new point of departure for the continuing debate. That debate has been supported on both sides by a phalanx of historians, members of Congress, academicians, current and former cabinet and subcabinet officers, and others.

In broad strokes the Constitution stipulates that the Congress shall have the power to declare war, to raise and support armies, and to provide and maintain a navy; the president shall be the commander in chief of the armed forces. The Constitutional Convention of 1787, hammering out the language on war powers, discussed granting Congress the power to "make war," but ultimately it decided on the power to "declare war," seemingly on the grounds that the conduct of war is an executive, not a congressional, function. Again in broad strokes, the War Powers Resolution of 1973 requires the president (1) to consult with the Congress "in every possible instance" before U.S. armed forces enter hostilities or situations of imminent hostilities; (2) to report to the Congress within forty-eight hours when forces are so committed; and (3) to terminate the engagement within sixty days if Congress has not declared war or specifically authorized continued use of the armed forces. Finally, it allows Congress within those sixty days to direct the president to withdraw U.S. forces by a concurrent resolution passed by both houses, but not requiring the president's signature.

1

It should be noted that in the nineteenth century it became accepted practice, with relatively little objection, for the president to use American forces in limited actions, mainly in our own hemisphere. In the twentieth century, with its two world wars, with the peculiar new animal the undeclared war, with the Soviet commitment to global communism producing cataclysm on every continent, with the memories we all have of Korea, Vietnam, the Cuban missile crisis, and the Berlin airlift, with the troubles in Latin America and the Middle East, where in truth lie the security and best interests of the United States in the allocation of war powers?

To chart a course out of this difficulty, we have a distinguished panel: Representative Lee H. Hamilton, Democrat of Indiana, has been a member of Congress since 1965. He is a member of the House Foreign Affairs Committee and serves on the Permanent Select Committee on Intelligence. Senator Charles McC. Mathias, Jr., Republican and senior senator from Maryland, is a member of the Senate Foreign Relations Committee and is second ranking member of the Judiciary Committee. Representative Dick Cheney, Republican of Wyoming, served in the Ford administration as White House chief of staff. Elected to the Congress in 1978, Representative Cheney was chosen by his colleagues to serve as chairman of the House Republican Policy Committee. He is also a member of the House Committee on Interior and Insular Affairs. Lieutenant General Brent Scowcroft, before retiring from military service in the air force, served in the White House as President Ford's national security adviser. More recently General Scowcroft served as chairman of President Reagan's Commission on Strategic Forces. In 1981 he was codirector of AEI's project on American Vital Interests in Regions of Conflict.

Let us hear first the views of our thirty-eighth president on the War Powers Resolution and the problems of trying to sort out the prerogatives and responsibilities of the Congress and the executive. Remember, the act was passed over President Nixon's veto in 1973. Gerald Ford succeeded to the presidency in 1974 and almost immediately had to confront the issue of war powers. (See the remarks of President Gerald Ford in the appendix.)

I would pose the same question to each of the panelists: Has the world changed so radically in two hundred years that the Congress should attempt what our Founding Fathers were not willing to do in writing the Constitution, specifically to define and catalog the prerogatives and powers of the Congress and the executive in the exercise of war powers?

CHARLES MCC. MATHIAS, JR., U.S. senator (Republican, Maryland): I would take issue with the question as it is framed, because it seems to

2

War Powers and the Constitution

John Charles Daly, moderator

Dick Cheney
Lee H. Hamilton
Charles McC. Mathias, Jr.
Brent Scowcroft

with an appendix by Gerald R. Ford

Held on December 6, 1983
and sponsored by
the American Enterprise Institute
for Public Policy Research
Washington and London

The AEI Project, "A Decade of Study of the Constitution," of which publication of this Public Policy Forum transcript is one activity, has been funded in part by a grant from the National Endowment for the Humanities.

This pamphlet contains the edited transcript
of one of a series of AEI forums.
These forums offer a medium for
informal exchanges of ideas on current policy problems
of national and international import.
As part of AEI's program of providing opportunities
for the presentation of competing views,
they serve to enhance the prospect
that decisions within our democracy will be based
on a more informed public opinion.
AEI forums are also available on
audio and color-video cassettes.

AEI Forum 61

ISBN 0–8447–2248–0
Library of Congress Catalog Card No. 84–070313
Printed in the United States of America

me that the Congress is not doing anything novel at the end of two centuries, anything different from what the Founding Fathers contemplated. The authors of the Constitution made it very clear where the power over war and peace would rest. It is true that they made the president commander in chief of the armed forces, but they vested the decision on war and peace solely in the Congress of the United States. They gave the Congress the power to make rules and regulations for the governance of the armed forces, to make rules for captures on land or water, to issue letters of marque, authorizing a warlike act by private vessels. So the Constitution vests a panoply of power in the Congress that makes it clear that the founders wanted the Congress to control issues of war and peace. What the War Powers Resolution does is merely to implement in a modern framework what I believe to be a very clear constitutional purpose.

DICK CHENEY, U.S. representative (Republican, Wyoming): I take strong exception to the view of my friend and colleague Senator Mathias. I believe that the declaration of war is almost an outmoded concept under virtually any set of circumstances we can conceive of under which a president would decide to commit troops to combat. In many respects the War Powers Resolution is a legacy of the Vietnam War, very much like the Trade and Neutrality Act of the late 1930s. It is a statute adopted in an effort to keep us out of the next war based on a misperception of how we got into the last one. It was put on the books with the expectation that if it had been on the books in 1964 and 1965, this nation would never have been involved in Southeast Asia. I believe that that is not the case. Congress consistently and continually supported our involvement in Southeast Asia, and the War Powers Resolution has not changed that. I believe very firmly that the War Powers Resolution is an unwise and virtually unworkable intrusion by the legislative branch into the powers and prerogatives the president needs to lead the United States in a very dangerous and hostile world.

LEE H. HAMILTON, U.S. representative (Democrat, Indiana): I support the War Powers Resolution. Edward Corwin, the great constitutional scholar, said that the Constitution is an invitation to the Congress and the president to struggle for the privilege of conducting American foreign policy. The War Powers Resolution simply reflects that struggle. Its purpose is to guarantee that the Congress and the president will exercise their collective judgment on the most important question faced by government, and that is whether or not the country goes to war. The extreme complexity of the modern world, the very rapid growth of America's responsibilities in that world, and the ambiguity of many international conflicts demand that the Congress and the

3

president exercise their collective judgment on the critical question of whether or not to go to war. To put the matter succinctly, in this kind of a world Lebanon is not Pearl Harbor, and when a decision calls for the best that we can summon, it ought not to be made by one man or woman, even if that man or woman is the president of the United States. It ought to be a collective judgment.

BRENT SCOWCROFT, lieutenant general–retired (U.S. Air Force): It is not so much that the world has changed in two hundred years as that the United States and its role in the world have changed substantially. The Constitution did not legislate a government designed for maximum efficiency. It legislated a government designed to protect the rights of the individual against an overweening government, and it does that very well. The problem is that the inefficiency that kind of freedom-protecting innovation dictates makes it very difficult for a world power to discharge its responsibilities.

As Representative Hamilton stated, in the struggle between the executive and the legislature for predominance, the balance has shifted throughout our history from one to the other. The War Powers Resolution reflects a time when, after a series of dynamic and activist presidents, the presidency was beset both by our involvement in Vietnam and by Watergate. The Congress in effect seized an opportunity to change the balance that had prevailed essentially since the administration of Franklin Roosevelt. We must find ways for the executive and the legislature to cooperate in the discharge of the awesome business of conflict, but I think the War Powers Resolution, in the way it attempts to achieve that, ties the hands of the president and makes conflict more likely.

SENATOR MATHIAS: I agree with Representative Cheney that the War Powers Resolution grew out of the experience of Vietnam. I lived through that as a member of Congress. I voted for the Gulf of Tonkin resolution, and I think it is fair to say that most of us who did vote for it felt, as the facts were revealed, that we had been bamboozled and that there was no mechanism by which the Congress could come to grips with the situation once the resolution had been passed. Once when I was riding in an automobile with President Johnson and expressed some doubts about the war, he said, "You voted for this resolution: now, if you've got the guts, step up and introduce a resolution to repeal it." And he reached in his pocket and pulled out a copy. We were really without a way to debate the issues; once troops are committed and casualties are being sustained and the patriotism of the country is aroused, it is very hard to get hold of.

The War Powers Resolution provides a mechanism and a process by which the Congress can periodically review our involvement in foreign military ventures. I think this is entirely consistent with what the writers of the Constitution proposed. James Madison, who probably knew more about the Constitution than any other man who ever lived, once wrote to Thomas Jefferson that the Constitution assumes what the history of all governments demonstrates: that the executive is the branch of power most interested in war and most prone to it. It has accordingly, with studied care, vested the question of war in the legislature.

REPRESENTATIVE CHENEY: I have to take exception to Senator Mathias. I think the War Powers Resolution—

SENATOR MATHIAS: You can take exception to me, but you would have trouble taking exception to Madison.

REPRESENTATIVE CHENEY: Obviously there are differences in our interpretations of what the Constitution provides with respect to whether the president or the legislature has prime authority in war powers. I think most members of Congress, even those like me who have serious problems with the War Powers Resolution, believe that the language of the resolution, which speaks of consultation and notification, is perfectly appropriate. It is the notion that Congress can terminate a commitment of forces after a very short period that bothers me a great deal.

I look on the Congress as all too often swayed by the public opinion of the moment. There is no procedure that would enable Congress to be an equal partner with the president, in light of all the resources available to him, in making broad policy decisions that must hold for a year or two. We have seen, for example, the Speaker of the House at the outset call the Grenada mission "gunboat diplomacy"; within two weeks he had changed his mind and concluded that President Reagan had done exactly the right thing in sending troops into Grenada.

SENATOR MATHIAS: He was right the first time.

REPRESENTATIVE CHENEY: Unfortunately Congress is a pretty weak reed to lean on for that kind of decision making. I would also argue that if the War Powers Resolution had been on the books in 1964 when the Gulf of Tonkin resolution was adopted, it would not have altered the outcome at all. Congress did indeed have the opportunity throughout our involvement in Southeast Asia to reject the course we were engaged on, but year after year it appropriated the funds for that exercise. I think it is a misreading of history to suggest that the War

5

Powers Resolution might have altered the outcome in Southeast Asia.

REPRESENTATIVE HAMILTON: I think the real question is whether a decision about war making ought to be made by one person or by the president and the Congress together. That seems to me to be at the heart of it, and the War Powers Resolution simply says that the Congress is going to participate in such a decision. Why shouldn't it? The guiding principle is that a democracy should go to war only with the consent of the people, as expressed by their elected representatives. So I think the War Powers Resolution is wholly consistent with the Constitution and with the intentions of the Founding Fathers. General Scowcroft spoke about tying the hands of the president. Quite frankly, that is one of the things we want to do. We want to make the president stop, think, and listen before he commits us to war.

REPRESENTATIVE CHENEY: The most important decision that anyone is going to make about the use of our military forces would obviously be a decision to use nuclear weapons. At that point Congress, even under the War Powers Resolution, is irrelevant. We have made a decision to build those weapons and to give the president as commander in chief control of them; if he decided tomorrow, because of an impending Soviet attack, to launch those weapons, Congress would have no role whatsoever. I think the idea of Congress sharing in the decision to declare war under such circumstances is almost meaningless.

REPRESENTATIVE HAMILTON: There may always be an emergency. The president may be faced with a decision when he has been told by his staff that the missiles are coming and he has only ten or fifteen or twenty minutes to respond. Clearly that would be an emergency. I do not think anyone would deny that the president ought to act then without trying to find the Speaker of the House or the majority leader of the Senate. But in an ordinary situation he ought to consult with the Congress before he goes to war. I believe that the War Powers Resolution is beneficial because it brings Congress into the decision on war, something it does not like to face.

REPRESENTATIVE CHENEY: Is there a recent example of a president's failing to consult before committing troops?

REPRESENTATIVE HAMILTON: Look what happened with Grenada. The president called in the Speaker and the majority leader at 8:00 P.M. He did not consult with them. The Speaker has said they were informed that the marines were landing at 5:30 the next morning. There was no consultation; it was just a matter of informing, and informing is not consultation. At 8:00 P.M. the Speaker learned about it, the rest of us learned about it from the newspaper, and the marines went in at 5:30. That is not consultation. When President Carter sent the troops to Iran for a rescue mission, he did not consult with the Congress. He just went ahead and did it.

REPRESENTATIVE CHENEY: It might have cost hundreds of lives if we had had the usual dialogue and debate about whether Congress would authorize action.

GENERAL SCOWCROFT: If we could broaden the discussion beyond the Congress, there are a number of other elements to consider. I want to underscore what Representative Cheney says: the Congress already has adequate resources to restrain the president. It does control the purse strings; it does raise and maintain armies. If it does not like what the executive is doing, it has all the power it needs to stop the president's actions.

REPRESENTATIVE HAMILTON: That is a very slow power; it takes Congress a long time to do that. The advantage of the War Powers Resolution is that, within the sixty-day period or the extended ninety-day period, the Congress has to act to approve or disapprove.

GENERAL SCOWCROFT: No, it does not have to act. That is one of the key points. If it does not act, it makes a decision by its inaction. That seems to me a supine way for the Congress to work its will. In the real world the president sometimes has to introduce forces into an area to try to prevent a conflict, to stabilize a region, or to prevent something from happening by demonstrating our resolve. Telling our potential opponents that all they have to do is wait sixty days and see what happens undercuts his ability to demonstrate the kind of resolve that could prevent a conflict.

REPRESENTATIVE HAMILTON: I disagree with that, General, because the act strengthens the decision to commit troops. If the president commits troops and does not have the support of the Congress or of the American people, he will not be able to sustain that commitment, and he will not be able to keep those troops there. We have learned that lesson very, very hard. How does he get the support of the American people? One of the ways is to have the support of the Congress.

MR. DALY: Let me ask you to focus on Lebanon. Senator Mathias, you played a major part in a compromise that was worked out, the terms of which were never specific, on whether the War Powers Resolution should apply to the president's commitment of marines to the peace-keeping force in Lebanon. That is a peculiar framework to consider because the president did not introduce troops into Lebanon to engage in hostilities but to join in a peace-keeping force with other nations. How do we address that situation?

SENATOR MATHIAS: Let me first add a footnote to Representative Cheney's comment that consulting Congress would bring about thousands of deaths because Congress cannot keep a secret. I very much disagree. In the Grenada situation the lack of consultation was compounded by the president's decision to advise the prime minister of Great Britain before he advised the Speaker of the House of Representatives and the majority leader of the Senate. That really causes me some trouble.

But to get down to Lebanon. I think the War Powers Resolution made a very positive contribution—though far from perfect—to the management of the Lebanese situation. There were some ambiguities both in the way the situation came about and in the structure of our response. But we made it very clear in the compromise that the troops on the beach were to be limited to the number who were there on the day the resolution passed. There were ambiguities about offshore naval forces, but there was absolutely no question about the troops on the beach; it was totally specific. We are protected from the kind of insidious growth that occurred in Vietnam, where we went from a few hundred advisers to 500,000 troops with only a kind of indirect congressional authorization: Congress provided their pay and their rations and thereby indirectly authorized their presence. But if we go beyond the number of Marines who were originally in Lebanon, there has to be real congressional consultation, more than just advice.

REPRESENTATIVE HAMILTON: Mr. Daly, did you say that the War Powers Resolution was not implemented in the Lebanon situation?

MR. DALY: No, I said that there seems to be some confusion about whether or not it was applied or is accepted as applied by both Congress and the president.

REPRESENTATIVE HAMILTON: It is very clear in the resolution that was passed that section 4A1 of the War Powers Resolution was implemented. President Reagan, when he signed it, did show some reservations; he obviously had some question about it, but he did sign it. This was the first full use of the War Powers Resolution as I understand it.

GENERAL SCOWCROFT: It seems to me that, with respect to Lebanon,

8

the question is not that clear. Legislation has been passed and agreed to and so on, but section 4A expressly talks about forces introduced. Those forces originally went in without any idea that hostilities were imminent. That hostilities or the possibility of hostilities subsequently developed seems to me to point to a very different kind of legal question.

REPRESENTATIVE HAMILTON: The War Powers Resolution permits the president or the Congress to trigger the section of the act concerning the sixty-day limit. In this case the Congress triggered it, started the time clock ticking, and the president accepted that. That stands as a historical precedent of major importance—for a president to accept the War Powers Resolution.

GENERAL SCOWCROFT: He did not accept the War Powers Resolution.

REPRESENTATIVE HAMILTON: The president accepted it by signing the Lebanon resolution. He made a statement about his reservations, but he signed the resolution, and it is the law of the land. The law specifically triggers the War Powers Resolution.

GENERAL SCOWCROFT: Representative Hamilton, many presidents have signed many bills while stating that there are constitutional problems. That does not mean that the president acquiesces.

REPRESENTATIVE CHENEY: That two such obviously intelligent and distinguished gentlemen as General Scowcroft and Representative Hamilton cannot even agree on what we did in the Lebanon resolution strikes me as pretty hard evidence that the War Powers Resolution is a very difficult piece of legislation and probably unworkable. I would certainly support General Scowcroft's views on what the administration did. I was fascinated by the debate on the issue when it came to the floor of the House because the debate had nothing to do with whether we should be there. Nobody offered an alternative that said everybody out now. The alternatives were 60-day, 90-day, 180-day, or eighteen-month limits, and often the debate over how long it should be had very little to do with the substance of the policy and much more to do with the posturing of my colleagues and whether anyone could build a majority for six months instead of nine months. It is a bad way to make policy. I also think the limit on numbers of troops on the beach is very unwise. If we are going to commit military force in a potentially hostile situation, one of the keys to its having any effect is the uncertainty created in the minds of our adversaries. If we say at the outset that we are going to commit troops but can have no more than 1,600 on the beach under any foreseeable circumstances, it defeats the purpose of having troops there in the first place.

SENATOR MATHIAS: Two points. One is the time factor. Of course, we are not talking about an absolute termination of the operation but about a period of time after which the Congress will make a review and there will be further consultation and, as Lee Hamilton says, a joint decision by the Congress and the executive whether the operation should be continued. That is a point that never came in Vietnam in a formal, structured way, and that is what was missing in the Vietnam debate. The executive could simply roll over the Congress. In fact, my good friend and colleague Mel Laird, who was secretary of defense, once said he did not even need appropriations, he could use the Food and Forage Act and just keep going without appropriations. That kind of experience makes some periodic congressional review desirable. I thought that six months was about the right time limit.

The other point I want to make is this. As Representative Cheney says, if we say we are going to get out in a limited time, that may make the adversary procrastinate and not come to terms with reality. In the Lebanese situation, however, not having a limit could make our friends there rest on their arms and not really engage in the hard political process necessary to bring about a reconciliation of the conflict. The longer they keep us there, the longer they do not have to come to terms with the reality of political life there. So there are two sides to the question of the uncertainties created by having or not having a time limit.

MR. DALY: What about the big constitutional question—the provision in the War Powers Resolution that gives Congress the right to direct the president to pull out even during the sixty-day period? Does it constitute, in effect, a legislative veto of his actions of the kind the Supreme Court held unconstitutional? Is the constitutional question here one that needs to be determined in the near term if we are to have an end to this debate?

REPRESENTATIVE CHENEY: I would like to relate an anecdote to the group on that point. I had the opportunity recently to travel in the Soviet Union. At one point I was pinned in an aircraft with two high Soviet officials who grilled me for three hours on the significance of the *Chadha* decision, which struck down the legislative veto, and what it meant for the implementation of the War Powers Resolution. Their conclusion after having studied it at least as closely as most American politicians was that indeed the president has far more authority and flexibility to commit troops in the future than he had in the past. I do not want to look to the Soviet Union for interpretation of our Constitution, but it is important and noteworthy that our primary adversary has good knowledge of that decision and interest in it. The decision that the Court handed down does not bode well for the legislative veto features of the War Powers Resolution, and the provision that would require the president to act by a simple majority vote of both houses of Congress is indeed a violation of separation of powers.

REPRESENTATIVE HAMILTON: I agree with Representative Cheney that the provision of the War Powers Resolution that permits the Congress to order the troops pulled out through a concurrent resolution is highly suspect in light of the Supreme Court decision. It is probably unconstitutional. There is a separability clause in the War Powers Resolution, however, and the balance of the resolution might still stand.

SENATOR MATHIAS: This anecdote of an experience on a Russian aircraft reminds me of a conversation with Marshal Ogarkov, a member of the Soviet armed forces. He was extremely interested in whether we were really going to dig 2,600 holes in the ground for the MX, as discussed during a previous incarnation of that debate. The interesting thing is how much high Soviet officials know about what is going on in America, and the depressing thing is how little high American officials know about what is going on in the Soviet Union. That is a point we ought to take to heart.

The question of the *Chadha* decision and whether the legislative veto is a problem does not affect a large part of the War Powers Resolution. The original statutory sixty-day limit on the use of troops overseas is not affected by the Supreme Court decision. That is untouched. The provisions on the growth of forces and the change of mission and the change of scope of the mission are untouched by the Supreme Court decision. It is just one rather narrow issue that is in question. Senator Javits, the author of the War Powers Resolution, feels very strongly that the original constitutional powers on which the resolution was founded are broad enough to raise the resolution and its legislative veto provision above the level of the *Chadha* decision, and I think that is at least an arguable case.

GENERAL SCOWCROFT: It seems to me that the legislative veto provision is only one of several items where the constitutionality of the resolution is at best dubious. It is quite clearly counter to the Constitution.

MR. DALY: Would you briefly review that decision for us, Senator?

SENATOR MATHIAS: It deals with the so-called legislative veto: Congress passes a statute and the president signs it, but the statute says that if the Congress does not like the way the executive is executing or applying it, one house of the Congress or, in some cases, both houses can pass a resolution without the president's signature that suspends that practice. In the *Chadha* decision the Court said we must follow the constitutional process of having legislation passed by both houses and signed by the president.

MR. DALY: It has been suggested that there should be an institutionalized mechanism for confrontation between the executive and the legislature, some supercommittee of the Congress as a counterpart to the National Security Council, which would serve as an information system for the Congress. Another suggestion is to have members of the Congress sit on the National Security Council. Do these approaches interest any of you?

REPRESENTATIVE CHENEY: There is obviously a need for consultation and notification. We will always have a debate over whether or not consultation was adequate. One of the difficulties the president has when he tries to consult with the Congress is that not everybody in the Congress agrees that he has consulted with the right people. Even though President Reagan, for example, talked with the majority and minority leaders of the Congress before the Grenada invasion, a number of people, including some of my colleagues, will still say that was inadequate consultation. There will always be a debate over whether it ought to be ten or fifteen or fifty members who are consulted and over who has the authority to speak for the Congress under those circumstances.

We also run into a problem with respect to covert operations. In 1975 Congress and its committees had gone along with covert operations in Angola, but once the operations became public, Congress headed for the hills and adopted the Clark amendment and shut them down. No matter what kind of mechanism we set up, whether it is an executive committee of the Congress or a more regularized institutional arrangement with the elected leaders of the Congress, we always come back to the fact that nobody can really commit the entire Congress. When the president consults with a group from Congress, he always runs the risk that, even though the leaders may sign off, the troops may not follow.

REPRESENTATIVE HAMILTON: As General Scowcroft and Representative Cheney both say, on the point of consultation, the resolution is not clear; it is ambiguous. Just what is consultation? I believe that whether or not the resolution works depends less on its language than on the attitude with which the Congress and the executive branch approach it. If we have an attitude of mutual respect and good faith, this resolution will work. If we do not have that, it will not work, no matter what is written into it with regard to consultation. The issue is more one of respect and good faith between the two branches than of specific requirements about consultation. I have looked at some amendments spelling out more completely what consultation means; they may improve the resolution, although it is hard for me to see that they would improve it greatly.

MR. DALY: Would any of you look kindly on having members of Congress serve with the National Security Council?

SENATOR MATHIAS: I think that would cause real constitutional problems. We are committed to the philosophy of separation of powers, and I do not see how we could have that kind of overlap.

I do not find as much trouble with consultation. I think it was entirely proper for the president to call in the legislative leaders. The impropriety occurred not in the people who were chosen but in the fact that the president did not consult them. They were simply called to the Oval Office at 8:00 P.M. and told that the troops were under way and were going to hit the beach at 5:00 in the morning. That is not consultation. Of course, I have to admit that very often the process of consultation is frustrated within the Congress itself. I remember the late Senator John McClellan used to say, "They don't tell me secrets in order for me to tell them to somebody else." He used to do what Senator Hollings calls "squat on it." That of course does diffuse the value of consultation. What we need here is just common sense; when the majority leader of the Senate is told something, he knows the critical people who need that information, and he can share it with them. It will work if common sense prevails, but that seems to be in short supply.

REPRESENTATIVE CHENEY: Senator Mathias is trying to define what would have been acceptable in the case of Grenada, for example. We had a situation there in which the president believed American lives were at stake and the only way to rescue them was through his decision, within his prerogatives as commander in chief, to mount a military operation, where any prior notice might well have led to serious loss of life among civilians or military personnel. Under such circumstances, when the whole train of events lasts only a few days from the time the trouble arises until the action is taken, what is acceptable consultation?

SENATOR MATHIAS: I'll tell you exactly. There were critical decisions being made down on the golf course in Atlanta. If the president really wanted to have a consultation, he could have said, "Tip, come down here and play a round of golf with me," and the Speaker could have joined in those conversations. I think it comes back to Representative Hamilton's statement that it is the spirit in which consultation takes place that is important.

REPRESENTATIVE CHENEY: I was present the morning of the Grenada event when the president met with a larger group and with the bipartisan leadership at the White House. This was at the time the invasion was under way. Not one member of either party in the room, of some thirty members of the House and Senate, raised a question about the operation. But three days later the Speaker was publicly condemning the president for gunboat diplomacy. Ten days later, once he had all the facts, after he had sent a delegation down to look at what had happened in Grenada, he said, "Whoops, I was wrong; it was, indeed, a good operation." How does the president deal with that kind of situation if he is trying to use some kind of reasonable, rational decision-making process?

SENATOR MATHIAS: Let me give you a quick answer. He does not do it on the basis of one operation or one episode. There must be a continuous consulting climate in which there is an ability to exchange views, in which a member of Congress does not stand in awe of the president because he only sees him once in four years.

REPRESENTATIVE CHENEY: But isn't Grenada a classic example not of a decision to go to war but rather of a commander in chief's taking action to save American lives? Therefore, the War Powers Resolution should probably not apply at all.

REPRESENTATIVE HAMILTON: I don't think so. After all, we committed combat troops in a very major way; those combat troops met resistance; they were fired on and sustained casualties; we had people killed in war, in the invasion or rescue operation, whatever you want to call it. The fact that the American people and, I think, the Congress strongly supported the action is not the relevant point. There was a period when the president was in the process of deciding whether we should go into Grenada. If we had the right kind of spirit prevailing, the right kind of consultation would be to invite the congressional leadership in—and no member of Congress could complain if the leaders invited were of both parties and both houses of the Congress— and say, "This is what I am thinking about doing." The important

14

point is prior consultation. In Grenada the order to invade had already been made; the president had signed that order before the 8:00 P.M. meeting. He did not call those leaders in to consult; he had already made up his mind to commit American troops for combat, and he did not consult with the leaders of Congress.

REPRESENTATIVE CHENEY: If he had consulted, what might have been the outcome?

REPRESENTATIVE HAMILTON: I don't know, but he has to give Congress the opportunity to be heard. These are tough questions. Maybe the question is not as tough in the Grenada situation as it would be in many others. The principle is that the most important decision government makes is whether or not to go to war. Should that decision be made by one person, or should it be made both by that person, the president, and by the Congress?

MR. DALY: During the debate about the division of war powers that began essentially in 1950 and ran through the 1960s and 1970s, there were people who disagreed strongly with the War Powers Resolution on the grounds that it gives the president powers that are not his under the Constitution. The thread ran continually through the debate that a War Powers Resolution meant to control the president does harm by giving him more powers than he has under the Constitution. Does that argument carry weight with you?

SENATOR MATHIAS: I don't think the War Powers Resolution alters the president's constitutional powers. They are what they are, and the War Powers Resolution does not change that. The argument you refer to is applied to the initial sixty-day period during which the president has an open license. Some people say that the Constitution does not give the president any days and therefore to say that a president can act during a sixty-day period without congressional authorization somehow enhances his power. I don't think it does. The sixty-day limit was a device built into the law in recognition of the kind of case where the president might have to act in an emergency to repel or to frustrate an invasion. The War Powers Resolution does not prevent the president from making foreign policy decisions. It simply says that they should be coordinated with the Congress, and under our system it is more efficient and effective to do that early.

GENERAL SCOWCROFT: I certainly agree that there should be consultation, and with the right spirit it can be worked out. The trouble is that with the right spirit we do not need the War Powers Resolution; with

15

the wrong spirit, the War Powers Resolution does not really affect the executive. Suppose a president consults as broadly as you want and the verdict is that he should not do something. There is nothing that prevents him from going ahead and doing it.

SENATOR MATHIAS: True—for a while.

GENERAL SCOWCROFT: For a while. For that while there is another clear issue of constitutionality: If the role of commander in chief does not include the right to move troops around, it is absolutely meaningless. The Congress arrogates to itself the right to force the president by its inaction to do something the Constitution says he does not have to do, to pull the troops out. By its own inaction, not even by telling the president he should not continue the action for some reason but just because it is unable to make up its own mind, it forces the president to behave other than as the commander in chief.

REPRESENTATIVE HAMILTON: The war-making powers are clearly divided in the Constitution. It does not give all the power to the president or all the power to the Congress. It is a shared power, and that is all we are trying to say in the War Powers Resolution. When we make a decision to go to war, let us make sure it is a shared, collective judgment.

GENERAL SCOWCROFT: But it was shared before. Take the Cooper-Church amendments concerning Vietnam, to cut off our use of military forces in and over Cambodia and so on. There are many ways for the Congress to insert into legislation the restrictions they feel are important, and without an item veto the president is stuck with them.

SENATOR MATHIAS: General, let me present a hypothetical situation to you. Do you think that the power of the commander in chief is so broad that the president of the United States could direct naval vessels with marines aboard to sail into the Gulf of Finland and order them to land in Leningrad, regardless of the opposition they might face, without any authorization from the Congress?

GENERAL SCOWCROFT: I suspect he could, yes. And I think that is not very dissimilar to what President Jefferson did against the Barbary pirates.

SENATOR MATHIAS: Knowing that was going to provoke World War III, do you think that would be within the power of the president?

16

GENERAL SCOWCROFT: The president can do a number of things that could under some circumstances provoke World War III, but that is a bizarre, extreme example. I cannot conceive of any president that any of us have known contemplating anything like that.

SENATOR MATHIAS: In the twenty years I have been in the Congress, I have witnessed things that I could never have conceived of the day I arrived.

MR. DALY: We have covered this subject very broadly, and I think it is time for the question-and-answer session. May I have the first question, please?

ROBERT LOCKWOOD, Pentagon: My question is directed to Representative Hamilton, who has done much work on improving the process of consultation between the executive and legislative branches. In light of the background and material and information he has collected over the years, we could all benefit from his views on what is available to the president to conduct operations of humanitarian rescue such as the Grenada incident.

REPRESENTATIVE HAMILTON: The authority is not in the War Powers Resolution, although that has been one of the suggestions for an amendment to the act. It is broadly accepted that one of the powers that attend a commander in chief is to protect American citizens and to rescue them. So far as I know, the authority of a president to go into a Grenada situation to rescue Americans is simply an extension of his powers as commander in chief.

SENATOR MATHIAS: When we are talking about what authority the president has in such a situation, we ought also to look at what inhibitions there are to his authority. If I had been in the meeting that Representative Cheney described, I would certainly have asked a question about the inhibitions imposed by the Treaty of Rio—signed by members of the Organization of American States—in which there is a clear prohibition against intervention by force.

GENERAL SCOWCROFT: But don't you think those questions were raised in the debate within the executive branch?

SENATOR MATHIAS: I hope so, but I don't know.

GENERAL SCOWCROFT: I can assure you that they were and that such decisions are not made lightly. Anybody can profit by wider consultation, but to imagine that only one man is making a decision is really an exaggeration. The process involves the entire executive branch, which considers options and pros and cons; they might come up with the wrong answer, no question about that.

SENATOR MATHIAS: We are sure that was true when you were the president's national security adviser, but I would feel better if that consultation were repeated with the legislative branch.

REPRESENTATIVE CHENEY: There comes a time, doesn't there, Senator, when somebody has to make a decision? When Jimmy Carter was president, I was not very pleased with his style of operation or the quality of the decisions made in his administration. But for the time a president is the constitutional president of the United States, he has the authority to make those kinds of decisions and judgments on behalf of all of us. If he makes a mistake, obviously we may pay a price for it; but we have to trust him to make certain decisions. To keep coming back to the notion that every set of circumstances in which military force might be used lends itself to consultation and legal arguments is nice, but the world doesn't work that way.

WALTER MUTHER, Associated Industries of Massachusetts: Representative Hamilton, given the consequences of the War Powers Resolution as I hear it interpreted, we had better have pretty quick wars to avoid the problem that congressional inaction could bring them to an end in sixty days. It is very hard to understand how that would be implemented, but that is what you say it stands for. Is that correct?

REPRESENTATIVE HAMILTON: I would say that to sustain a war requires the support of the Congress and the American people. They ought to be in on the takeoff decision; if they are not, the chances of the president's being able to sustain the war are not good. That is all we are seeking to do—to bring the Congress into that decision-making process.

GENERAL SCOWCROFT: Are you arguing that the Congress and the American people were not in on the takeoff in Vietnam? As I review the debate over the Gulf of Tonkin resolution, it seems quite clear what the potential of U.S. involvement was.

REPRESENTATIVE HAMILTON: I don't think I even mentioned the Vietnam War.

GENERAL SCOWCROFT: No, but that seems to me the implication of what you are saying, that somehow things have to be clear and, if they are, Congress and the American people will not bail out if things do not go well.

REPRESENTATIVE HAMILTON: If I were in the executive branch and were making such a weighty decision as the commitment of troops, I would want to know that the leaders of the Congress were going to support me.

GENERAL SCOWCROFT: I agree completely.

REPRESENTATIVE HAMILTON: If that is your feeling, how would you carry it out? It seems to me that you would at least call the leadership in and go over the matter in some detail before a final decision to commit troops.

GENERAL SCOWCROFT: That depends on the circumstances.

REPRESENTATIVE HAMILTON: I can envision circumstances when it is not possible to do that.

MR. DALY: Former Senator Frank Church, who was chairman of the Foreign Relations Committee, voted for the War Powers Resolution in 1973, but he is having second thoughts. He said, "If the president uses the armed forces in action that is both swift and successful, then there is no reason to expect the Congress to do other than applaud. If the president employs forces in an action that is swift but *unsuccessful*, then the Congress is faced with a *fait accompli* and, although it may rebuke the president, it could do little else. If the action is a foreign war that is large and sustained, the argument that the War Powers Resolution forces the Congress to confront that decision overlooks the fact that it has no other course to take. The Congress must appropriate the money to make it possible for this sustained action to be sustained." So I wonder whether we have done very much to further our purpose through the War Powers Resolution.

SENATOR MATHIAS: I think Frank Church said nothing more than Representative Hamilton has said here. The question is whether the resolution can be effective in having the best judgments made in the affairs of the American people. We are groping for means and mechanisms for arriving at the very best judgments that are humanly possible. The War Powers Resolution is not holy writ; it is a means by which we reach out for a better way to make decisions. We have made some bloopers over the years, and we would like to reduce the incidence of mistakes. Whether the act will ultimately be effective will depend on how we use it. We are in an evolutionary period in which the president and the Congress are interpreting it, and we may, as a result of this exercise, come up with a better way of doing business. I hope we will. Perhaps each side will have to give a little and adjust a little, but that is the traditional way of improving the body politic.

JOHN RALM, Clackamas Community College, Oregon City, Oregon: My question is for Representative Cheney. If the Supreme Court were to declare the War Powers Resolution of 1973 unconstitutional because it infringes upon the president's power to commit troops, what legislative alternatives would you propose?

REPRESENTATIVE CHENEY: My view is that we do not need the War Powers Resolution. If the Court strikes it down, I expect it would be on the basis that it constitutes a legislative veto: The president does not have the opportunity to veto an act of the Congress directing him to withdraw troops; it therefore violates the separation of powers. The heart of having the relations between the president and the Congress work is basically a requirement of good faith effort on both sides. My view is that Congress already has adequate means to set restrictions and restraints, and it has powers and authority to intervene if the president does make a serious mistake. It has the power of the purse and the opportunity to hold hearings and conduct oversight investigations and decide whether Congress wants to sustain an effort after the fact. In the 1980s and beyond we are very unlikely to find ourselves in circumstances where the kind of conflict envisioned in the War Powers Resolution is likely to arise. Presidents have to be trusted to some extent. Once they are elected, we delegate enormous authority to them directly and indirectly. We build nuclear weapons systems and give them total control over those systems without consultation with the Congress. Having made that leap of faith, we can trust the president to be commander in chief. There is no need for a replacement for the War Powers Resolution if it should be struck down.

SENATOR MATHIAS: There is a subjective value to the War Powers Resolution that perhaps has not been sufficiently appreciated. During the debate in which it was first adopted, Senator Javits used to say that it was like a sign at a railroad crossing, that it was simply saying, stop, look, and listen before embarking on this journey overseas. That is the effect we hoped it would have on the executive branch. But there is an important subjective effect on the legislative branch. In a nonadversarial way, the act provides a framework for examining an operation. When I introduced the resolution, in 1969, to repeal the Gulf of Tonkin resolution—I finally took up Lyndon Johnson's challenge—that was an adversarial action. But the periodic reviews that are provided for in the War Powers Resolution do not have to be adversarial. People will take sides within the debate, but the existence of the debate itself becomes a matter of procedure and is neutral.

GENERAL SCOWCROFT: I suggest that is not the way it is viewed by the executive branch. It is viewed as an irritant and considered as showing congressional intent to infringe on the prerogatives of the president. It prevents the cooperative consultation that I think is the fundamental answer to the problem.

REPRESENTATIVE CHENEY: I don't think we can find an example in modern times when a president has failed to do what the War Powers Resolution expects him to do about consultation and notification. I don't know of anybody who has served in the presidency in the last thirty or forty or fifty years or longer who would have made a decision in a highhanded fashion to commit troops in a way that ultimately lacked the broad public support such a decision requires. Certainly that was not Lyndon Johnson's intention when he got involved in Southeast Asia. Certainly that was not the intention of Congress when they supported that involvement. In the end public opinion swung against our involvement after years of developments and gradual, constant escalation, but nothing in the War Powers Resolution would have changed that. I think we do have to rely to some extent on good faith interpretation of our responsibilities both as legislators and as executives, and I think that has been there in virtually every case.

REPRESENTATIVE HAMILTON: Let me make an observation about the War Powers Resolution from the standpoint of the Congress. General Scowcroft talked about it from the standpoint of the executive branch, and I think his observation was accurate and correct.

From the standpoint of the Congress, it seems to me, the War Powers Resolution has had great symbolic importance as a reassertion of congressional authority. Those of us who served in the Congress right after Vietnam came out of that experience with a strong feeling that we had not done our job very well. The country had made a major decision that had not worked out well, and we were criticized very strongly. The War Powers Resolution grew out of that experience, and it passed the House and the Senate overwhelmingly. It was passed strongly over a presidential veto. It became very important for us symbolically.

The second thing I can say about it from the standpoint of the Congress is that it forces Congress to face the tough questions, such as, Are you going to leave the marines in Lebanon or not? Congress likes to duck tough questions; so maybe one beneficial aspect of this resolution is that it does make the Congress confront tough questions that it might otherwise avoid.

GENERAL SCOWCROFT: I agree with that except for the provision whereby it does allow the Congress to duck the question. By its inaction it forces the president to do something.

SENATOR MATHIAS: One of the reasons we are meeting is to discuss constitutionality; therefore, I drag you back to the history of the Constitution. The executive side of this argument is presented as the need to repose confidence in the judgment of the president and his advisers. Alexander Hamilton was never thought to be soft on the executive. He was always viewed as an advocate of a strong executive. In *The Federalist Papers,* however, he wrote, "The history of human conduct does not warrant that exalted opinion of human virtue which would make it wise in a nation to commit interests of so delicate and momentous a kind as those which concern intercourse with the rest of the world to the sole disposal of a magistrate created in circumstance as would be the President of the United States." There was a kind of concern expressed at the very birth of the republic that reflects the problems we are discussing here.

GENERAL SCOWCROFT: I agree with that, but to imagine that the world was so different that the framers did not know what they were doing is wrong. A recent study found that about 10 percent of the military engagements throughout the world between 1780 and 1880 were consequent to a declaration of war. So the idea that undeclared wars are a recent phenomenon—

SENATOR MATHIAS: The degree is different, but the circumstances are pretty standard.

GENERAL SCOWCROFT: In the process of writing the Constitution, the words "make war" were deliberately changed to "declare war." That cannot have been accidental, and that is a very important change. One is recognizing a situation; the other is initiating a situation.

SENATOR MATHIAS: But Hamilton, who was there, argues that the power was not vested solely in the president and should not have been.

GENERAL SCOWCROFT: And it is not, because the Congress raises and maintains armies.

ROBERT GOLDWIN, director of Constitutional Studies, American Enterprise Institute: Senator Mathias, the passage from Alexander Hamilton that you quoted was in reference not to making war or declaring war but to the Senate's power of constitutional "advice and consent" on treaties and appointments. That raises an interesting question related to what Representative Hamilton was saying about bringing Congress into decision making. Do you mean there should be congressional "consent" in the same sense as "advice and consent" with regard to treaties? That is, if you restrict the power of the president to the extent that he must consult with members of Congress, and they give him opposing or conflicting advice, what should the president do? Do you really mean that congressmen should have some part of the decision-making power? Wouldn't that put in real question the whole principle of separation of powers?

SENATOR MATHIAS: I think we made that clear in reference to the question about whether legislators should serve on the National Security Council. I think that clearly would be a violation of the separation of powers and under the American Constitution would not be proper. I am not suggesting that. I think what Hamilton was looking at was foreign policy, and war is, of course, the ultimate act of foreign policy. So I think war powers are clearly comprehended in his thinking. A coordinate decision must be made. I do not see how we can ever embody in a statute precisely how this will occur. Lee Hamilton has one kind of personality, and Dick Cheney has another; there will be presidents with whom one of them will be sympathetic and the other will not. General Scowcroft and Dick Cheney, both having served in the highest positions in the White House, know how personalities become important in policy making and execution, and that is one reason that it is impossible to create an absolutely rigid system of consultation, that from administration to administration it will change. But the president must be exposed to all the considerations *before* he makes a decision.

REPRESENTATIVE HAMILTON: You asked whether the Congress should consent—why shouldn't the Congress consent? What is wrong in a democracy about making a judgment in a democratic manner? That is all we are asking.

GENERAL SCOWCROFT: Should consent be mandatory? Should it be binding on the president?

23

REPRESENTATIVE HAMILTON: The question was whether the Congress should consent to the decision, and I see nothing wrong with that. What kind of a war can the president of the United States carry out if the Congress of the United States does not consent?

REPRESENTATIVE CHENEY: In many respects we have already given prior approval. We have appropriated the funds and raised the army and purchased the equipment and built the missiles and the bombers, and the president has the authority to make decisions about how to use those things. To suggest that the president can involve the Congress as deeply as I think you would like to in advance of the actual commitment of troops strikes me as not very practical.

SENATOR MATHIAS: I simply do not believe that the existence of the defense establishment is in some way an authorization to the president to start out on foreign adventures.

REPRESENTATIVE CHENEY: It is a recognition that we live in a dangerous and hostile world and from time to time may have to defend ourselves and our interests. We look to the president to make decisions that are naturally made by a commander in chief rather than a legislative body.

SENATOR MATHIAS: We entrust that final decision to the president, but we have confidence that the secretary of state and the secretary of defense will have some comment, that the Joint Chiefs of Staff will talk about the military feasibility, that the Central Intelligence Agency will provide basic information, that the whole apparatus of government will be brought to bear. At some point in that decision-making process—and I certainly did not mean to imply that this was something the president decides in the shower on his own—there is room and time to register the congressional point of view.

REPRESENTATIVE HAMILTON: We have to draw a distinction between two situations. One is an emergency. Representative Cheney, you refer to that frequently, and I think you are probably correct. There are going to be times when the president has to act. Do you believe that was true in Grenada, that American citizens had to be rescued right then, and the president really did not have time? I can see how you can make a case for the president moving very quickly. But that is not the only situation in which a president will be confronted with a decision to commit troops. Should we invade Nicaragua today? That is a possible question on the agenda of the country. If I were a president reflecting on that question today, I would call Senator Mathias and others and talk with them about it. That is what we are saying, and that kind of situation is very different from an emergency.

GENERAL SCOWCROFT: The War Powers Resolution does not say that the president will not attack this or that or the other. It says the president may not move troops, may not introduce troops in certain areas. That brings us back to Representative Cheney's point about having raised armies: What can the president do with them? If the commander in chief cannot deploy and move his forces around, the term "commander in chief" is absolutely meaningless. We are not talking about specifically going to war; there is nothing about that in the War Powers Resolution.

SENATOR MATHIAS: We are talking about hostilities, and that *is* in the War Powers Resolution.

GENERAL SCOWCROFT: Where it is possible. We are not talking about the president using forces offensively to attack.

TERRY EMERSON, office of Senator Barry Goldwater: I have a quick comment on Alexander Hamilton. In a famous set of written debates with James Madison, Hamilton made a clear distinction between offensive and defensive war. He said the Congress can commence offensive war through the declaration power but the president possesses the power to initiate defensive actions on behalf of the United States.

My question to the panel is whether any member would wish to test the War Powers Resolution against the history immediately preceding World War II. Take the actions of President Franklin Roosevelt in 1941. In 1940 Congress had renewed the military draft by a single vote. Yet in 1941, before any declaration of war, Roosevelt sent American marines equipped for combat to both Greenland and Iceland. He gave them orders to cooperate fully with British armed forces already there defending the islands against Nazi Germany. Roosevelt also ordered the American navy to escort British shipping in the North Atlantic and to shoot on sight German U-boats. All this before any declaration of war. Under the War Powers Resolution, Congress would have had to vote within sixty days on whether to extend President Roosevelt's powers. I ask whether the War Powers Resolution in that situation would not have led to a total disaster for the democracies of the world through an isolationist Congress's refusing to ratify President Roosevelt's wise actions.

REPRESENTATIVE CHENEY: The gentleman stated the case eloquently; I think he is absolutely right.

SENATOR MATHIAS: We can make only a hypothetical judgment about what might have happened if the War Powers Resolution had been in effect. It is difficult to say, given the unpredictability of history. Senator Goldwater, for example, voted against the War Powers Resolution but thereafter called for the immediate withdrawal of the marines from Lebanon. I don't know what real conclusions we can draw.

MR. DALY: This concludes another public policy forum presented by the American Enterprise Institute for Public Policy Research. On behalf of AEI, our hearty thanks to the distinguished and expert panelists, Representative Lee H. Hamilton, Senator Charles McC. Mathias, Jr., Representative Dick Cheney, and Lieutenant General Brent Scowcroft, and our thanks also to our guests and experts in the audience for their participation.

Appendix

Gerald R. Ford

Questions of war and peace, which are the responsibility of the president in the White House and of the Congress are too serious not to be of dual responsibility. From my practical experience in the Congress for twenty-five years and two and a half years in the White House, however, I thoroughly believe that trying to put on paper a precise procedure by which things have to be done in a crisis is impractical in the first place. Second, I believe it is unconstitutional since it undercuts a president's responsibility as commander in chief of our military forces. And third, the most important point, a president of the United States, under any and all circumstances, has to maximize his effort either to maintain the peace or, where there is no peace, to obtain it. I firmly believe, as a practical matter, that the War Powers Resolution with all its requirements handicaps a president in trying to achieve and maintain the peace.

Now let me take a specific example of what happened under the War Powers Resolution during my administration. I am sure people recall the seizure of the merchant vessel *Mayaguez* in 1975, when the Cambodians violated international law by seizing an American ship off the shores of Cambodia. That precipitated, of course, a challenge to my administration as to how we could get the crew back without any loss of life and how we could recover the ship itself. Under the War Powers Resolution, we would have been handicapped in trying to go through all of the procedures that were required. We had to take action, and we did; and the result was that the crew and ship were recovered from the enemy.

Now, that did not mean that we failed to consult with the Congress; we invited as many key congressmen and senators as we could find to the Cabinet Room. We informed them of the facts, and we outlined what we were going to do, which later turned out to be successful. But

NOTE: President Ford's comments were videotaped on December 7, 1983, and have been edited.

if we had been required to do this in a straight-jacketed way, we would have lost valuable time, we might not have been able to move as promptly and precisely as we did, and the crew of the *Mayaguez* might have suffered the same fate as the crew of the *Pueblo*, the American ship and crew seized by the North Koreans and held for some eighteen months. I was determined to avoid the *Pueblo* situation developing under any circumstances, so we moved rapidly. We consulted with the Congress, but we never conceded that the War Powers Resolution was applicable. If we had, we might have been delayed, we might have been hamstrung, and we might not have been successful.

I had my chief of congressional liaison with the Congress, Jack Marsh, and his assistants notify the congressional leadership, Democratic as well as Republican, that an American ship had been illegally seized. I also indicated some of the options we faced. We then invited the leadership of the House and Senate, Democrats as well as Republicans, to the White House for a meeting in the Cabinet Room where we had in attendance the secretaries of defense and state, the chairman of the joint chiefs of staff, and the director of the Central Intelligence Agency. A full briefing was presented. We went through the process of notification and giving information, but we did not concede that what we did was covered by the War Powers Resolution.

We made our decision based on what we felt was requisite military action and appropriate diplomatic action, since we were operating through diplomatic as well as military channels. The views of various congressional members were not based on the kind of indepth information that a president gets from his staff. Members of Congress have many other duties. Their principal responsibility is not to be commander in chief. Information as to what is transpiring during a crisis on a minute-by-minute or hour-by-hour basis, therefore, is not available to them.

A president, on the other hand, where the Constitution gives him the responsibility as commander in chief, has to know by the hour what's happening so that he can act in a responsible manner. You cannot have 535 commanders in chief. You cannot have 535 secretaries of state. Their duties, under our constitution are different—important but different, from the president's.

It is more difficult to bring the Congress into decision making during an emergency than it is on broader strategy, for example in planning a position for our government on a strategic arms limitation agreement. In the latter case, we have time. World events or tragedies do not always happen during the working hours of the Congress, even when Congress is in session, so you cannot write a textbook on how consultation should take place. A president ought to maximize his efforts to notify and to consult the Congress, but he cannot give away his re-